OPERATION EARTH
AIR SCARE

**by
Jeremy Leggett**

HEINEMANN

A Templar Book
First published in Great Britain in 1991
by Heinemann Children's Reference
A division of Heinemann Educational Books Ltd
Halley Court, Jordan Hill, Oxford OX2 8EJ
Devised and produced by The Templar Company plc
Pippbrook Mill, London Road, Dorking, Surrey RH4 1JE

Editors: Wendy Madgwick, Steve Parker
Designers: Jane Hunt, Sue Rawkins
Illustrator: Rod Ferring

Colour separations by Positive Colour Ltd, Maldon, Essex
Printed and bound by L.E.G.O., Vicenza, Italy

British Library Cataloguing in Publication Data

Leggett, Jeremy
Air scare.
1. Atmosphere. Pollution
I. Title   II. Series
363.7392

ISBN 0-431-00788-8

Whilst the contents of this book are believed correct at the time of going to
press, changes may have occurred since that time or will occur during
the currency of this book.

Photographic credits
t = top, b = bottom, l = left, r = right
page 6 Janet and Colin Bord/Wales Scene; *page 8* NASA/Science Photo Library;
page 10 European Space Agency/Science Photo Library; *page 13* Michael
Gilbert/Science Photo Library; *page 14* Anthony Bannister/NHPA; *page 15*
The Photo Source; *page 18* Dan Farber/Science Photo Library; *page 23 t,l*
Robert Harding Picture Library; *page 23 t,r* Daisy Blow/ICCE; *page 23 b,l* Robert
Harding Picture Library; *page 23 b,r* Kimball Morrison; *page 26* Simon
Fraser/Science Photo Library; *page 27* Thor Larsen/WWF; *page 28* Brian
Hawkes/NHPA; *page 28 inset* Dr Gener Feldman, NASA GSFC/Science Photo
Library; *page 29* Frane Lane/Holt Studios; *page 30* Sally and Richard Greenhill;
page 31 Mark N. Boulton; *page 36 t* Sally and Richard Greenhill; *page 36 b*
Simon Fraser/Science Photo Library; *page 39 t,l* François Gohier/Ardea;
page 39 t,r Ronald Toms/Oxford Scientific Films; *page 39 b,l* Lowell
Georgia/Science Photo Library; *page 40* Walter Rawlings/Robert Harding

CONTENTS

THE NATURE OF AIR

Every living thing on Earth needs to breathe air. Natural, clean air is vital for life.

The air on Earth forms our **atmosphere**. This is a sort of invisible "envelope" which covers the whole planet and is more than 400 kilometres thick. The atmosphere is made up of a natural mixture of gases, such as nitrogen and oxygen. The atmosphere, and the life it supports, have slowly changed or evolved together over hundreds of millions of years.

Today, there is an "Air Scare". We are changing the make-up or nature of our atmosphere. The changes will be disastrous if we do not do something to stop them. That is the bad news. The good news is that we are recognizing the problem and working out how to solve it. In recent years, people have taken the first steps towards repairing the atmosphere.

A NATURAL BALANCE
From the microscopic plant life of the sea to the giant American redwood, all plant life depends on clean air. Plants are responsible for keeping the levels of oxygen and carbon dioxide in the air constant. They also provide animals with food. They are at the centre of a delicate balance of Nature.

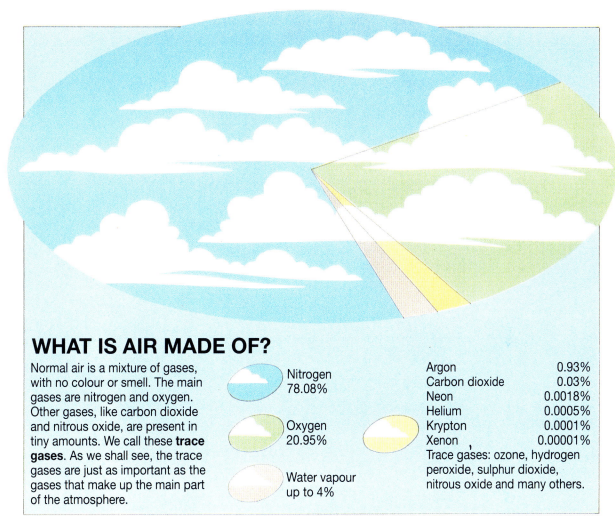

WHAT IS AIR MADE OF?

Normal air is a mixture of gases, with no colour or smell. The main gases are nitrogen and oxygen. Other gases, like carbon dioxide and nitrous oxide, are present in tiny amounts. We call these **trace gases**. As we shall see, the trace gases are just as important as the gases that make up the main part of the atmosphere.

Nitrogen 78.08%

Oxygen 20.95%

Water vapour up to 4%

Argon	0.93%
Carbon dioxide	0.03%
Neon	0.0018%
Helium	0.0005%
Krypton	0.0001%
Xenon	0.00001%

Trace gases: ozone, hydrogen peroxide, sulphur dioxide, nitrous oxide and many others.

AIR AND LIFE

Living things need the oxygen in air for a process called **respiration**. *In this, they get energy from food by adding oxygen to it. The oxygen is taken in from the air in animals by breathing and through tiny holes in the leaves of plants. Respiration uses up oxygen and makes carbon dioxide.*

As well as respiring, plants use another process, called **photosynthesis**. *So long as the Sun shines on them, they can take the gas carbon dioxide, and water, and make food from them. Photosynthesis uses up carbon dioxide and gives off oxygen.*

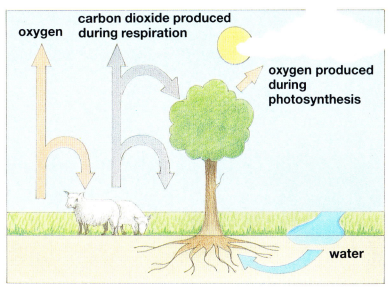

oxygen

carbon dioxide produced during respiration

oxygen produced during photosynthesis

water

EARTH'S ATMOSPHERE

Our atmosphere is almost as old as our planet, and it has gradually changed over millions of years. In the beginning, it was very different from the atmosphere we know today. It was poisonous to life.

The Earth formed 4600 million years ago. The first signs of life are shown by fossils in rocks 3500 million years old. Early life was mainly bacteria (microscopic living things) and simple small plants called algae. These were found only in the sea. The Sun's rays were too strong for life to exist on land, and there was much more carbon dioxide in the atmosphere than there is today.

About 2000 million years ago, oxygen began to build up in the atmosphere. By 400 million years ago, the ozone layer (see page 26) had built up enough to protect the land's surface from the Sun's damaging **ultraviolet** rays or **radiation**. The first land plants and animals soon appeared. Within a few tens of millions of years, great forests grew up. There was a huge expansion of life on land, and the atmosphere gradually took on its present-day form.

WHAT THEY SAY

"The pale blue pearl in space" … When American astronauts went to the Moon, they were amazed to see how small and isolated the Earth seemed in the vastness of space. Soviet astronauts said that they could not see the boundaries of different countries from space. All people share the same living place.

THE LAYERS OF THE ATMOSPHERE

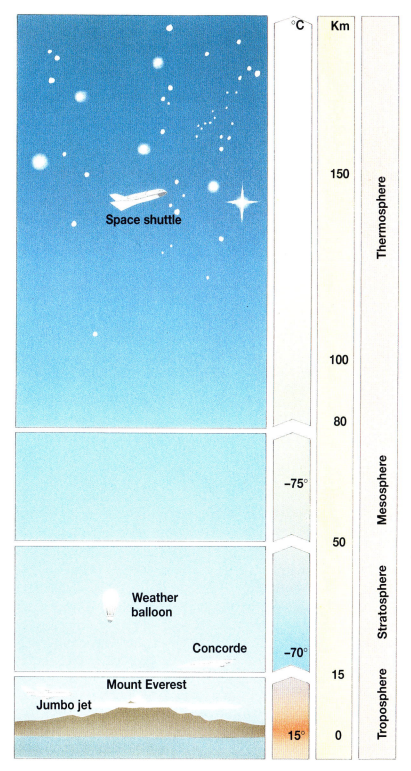

°C | Km

Thermosphere

150

100 — 80

−75° — 80 **Mesosphere**

Space shuttle

Weather balloon

Concorde — −70°

Mount Everest

Jumbo jet — 15° — 15 / 0

Stratosphere

Troposphere

Thermosphere (80-400 kms)
About 400 kilometres up in the **thermosphere**, the atmosphere has almost disappeared. It is replaced by space, where there is no air.

Mesosphere (50-80 kms)
The air is even thinner and colder in the **mesosphere**, with temperatures down to −75°C.

Stratosphere (15-50 kms)
In this layer the air is much thinner than in the troposphere. There is less of all the gases, and much less water vapour. The **stratosphere** contains the ozone layer, which stops many of the Sun's harmful ultraviolet rays from reaching the surface of the planet.

Troposphere (0-15 kms)
This is the zone in which clouds and weather occur. It becomes colder as you go upwards. The average temperature on the Earth's surface is 15°C. At the top of the **troposphere**, in a boundary called the tropopause, it may be −70°C.

9

TEMPERATURE
AND CLIMATE

WEATHER PATTERNS

Weather satellites orbit the Earth taking photographs of weather patterns. This one of Europe shows that there are storms over the UK, with dense clouds over parts of Scandinavia. This false colour image is produced by a computer. It helps to make the land and weather systems easier to see.

The Sun's rays warm the Earth, and create our **weather** and **climate**. "Weather" describes what temperatures, clouds and winds do over a short time, from hours to days and weeks. "Climate" describes what they do over longer periods, from years to centuries.

The weather is very complicated. It depends on many factors, such as air pressure, temperature and the amounts of water vapour in the atmosphere. As we know, it is difficult to determine or predict what the weather will be like even a few days in the future! Yet,

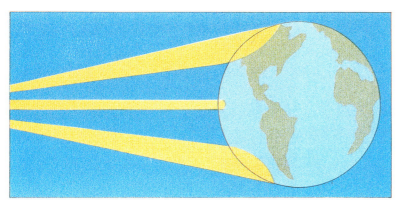

TEMPERATURE ZONES

The Sun's rays hit the surface of the Earth at different angles. At the Equator, they come directly downwards, and so the surface is very warm. Farther north or south, they hit the Earth at a more glancing angle, and their warming effect is weaker. This difference in heating is the main reason why the climate varies from one region of the Earth to another.

Average yearly temperatures

Equator 27°C	Tropics 23°C	Subtropics 20°C	Temperate zone 17°C	Polar zone 5°C

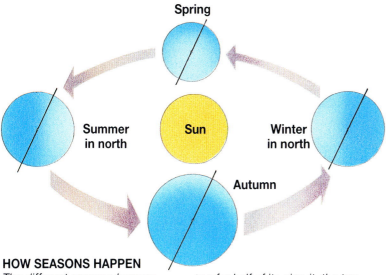

Spring

Summer in north

Sun

Winter in north

Autumn

HOW SEASONS HAPPEN

The different seasons happen because of the way the Earth goes round the Sun. Its circuit is not round. Also, the Earth is tilted, and so for half of its circuit, the top part is nearer the Sun. It is summer in the north. As the circuit continues, it becomes summer in the south.

because we have weather records going back many years, we can predict the general climate. For example, North Africa tends to have hot, dry summers, while Northern Europe usually has warm, damp summers.

Humans can survive a great range of temperatures, from the hottest desert to the cold South Pole. We do this by making buildings for shelter, and by wearing clothes. However, the natural world can cope only with a small temperature range. If the climate changes too quickly, it may badly affect plants and animals.

GREEN LAND?

Hundreds of years ago, Greenland was much warmer. When Erik and his Vikings first settled there (see page 17), it was indeed a "green land", with trees and plants. Then it became colder quite quickly, as part of the natural climate cycle. Many trees, plants and animals could not adapt or change, and they died out. The same thing can happen if an area or region becomes hotter too quickly.

THREE PROBLEMS

In 1988, the Canadian Government organized a world meeting about the atmosphere and its pollution. More than 300 experts came, from 48 countries. They described the way we are altering the atmosphere as "an uncontrolled experiment". They also said that it could have bad effects which would be "second only to global nuclear war".

The experts described three main threats. These are the **greenhouse effect**, **acid rain**, and the loss of **ozone**.

Since that meeting, many leaders have agreed that there is a problem, which must be dealt with quickly. President Bush of the USA promised to use his influence and power to help – the "White House effect". President Gorbachev of the USSR spoke of his belief that large amounts of money, now spent on weapons, must instead be spent on repairing the atmosphere.

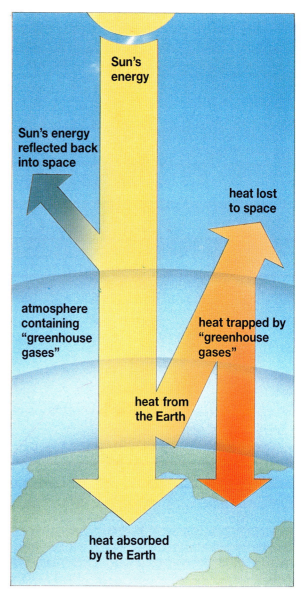

WHAT ARE WE DOING?
● Many countries have made an agreement to try to slow down the loss of ozone. It is called the Montreal Protocol, and was signed by 46 countries in 1987.
● Over 80 governments are ready to sign a new, stronger agreement. Scientists believe that even this will not stop the ozone loss.
● Some countries have agreed to reduce the fumes that produce acid rain.
● Governments have so far only discussed the greenhouse effect. Some countries want to act by signing an agreement called a Global Climate Convention.

THE GREENHOUSE EFFECT
(see pages 14-21)

Greenhouse glass lets through the Sun's rays. Inside, some of the rays are changed when they **reflect** off the objects there. The glass does not let these rays out, but traps them as heat. The inside of the greenhouse warms up. This is happening to the Earth. Certain trace gases, which we have added to the atmosphere, trap heat from the Sun's rays as it is reflected from the Earth's surface. The greenhouse effect is also known as **global warming**.

gases like sulphur dioxide and nitrogen dioxide dissolve in rain water to make acid rain

ACID RAIN
(see pages 22-25)

Acids are **corrosive** – they eat away or dissolve objects. When you suck a lemon, you are tasting a weak acid. Some trace gases, which we have added to the atmosphere, cause rain and snow to be more acidic than they would be naturally. The rain falls to the ground and makes the soil and water more acidic, too. This harms animals and plants. Acid rain has killed countless fish, while large areas of forest are now full of sick or dying trees.

LOSS OF OZONE
(see pages 26-29)

The ozone layer (shown here as a white layer) is about 20-30 kilometres high, in the stratosphere (see page 9). In 1985, scientists found a huge "hole" in the ozone layer over Antarctica (white landmass). The next year they discovered that some trace gases, which we have added to the atmosphere, are destroying ozone. Soon they found ozone loss in other areas, too. More harmful radiation is now getting through to the Earth's surface (purple rays), and there is a danger to living things.

THE WORLD HEATS UP

The Sun's rays consist of several kinds of radiation. Some are harmful, like ultraviolet radiation (see page 8). Some pass through the atmosphere to heat the world. These include light rays or **visible radiation** (so called because our eyes can see it).

The rays from the Sun warm the surface of the planet. The warm surface gives off **infrared** (heat) radiation which is reflected upwards, towards space. Not all of the reflected rays can pass back through the atmosphere. Certain trace gases, known as greenhouse gases, absorb this extra infrared radiation and the atmosphere warms up.

(see page 8)

THE ROLE OF THE SEA

Many, many things affect global warming and each one affects many of the others. It is a very difficult puzzle for the scientists. For example, the oceans (see right) cover two-thirds of the Earth. How will they react? At the moment they soak up, or absorb, a lot of carbon dioxide. As the Earth heats up, so will the oceans. Will they still be able to absorb so much carbon dioxide? Many scientists suspect not. This would make the greenhouse effect more severe.

HOW HOT, AND HOW LONG?

Scientists are using the world's most powerful computers to predict global warming. It is difficult because Nature is so complicated. Their work seems to show that the Earth's average temperature will rise by about 3°C, over the next 50 to 100 years – unless we stop putting artificial greenhouse gases into the atmosphere.

A WORLD OF DESERTS?

In many arid (very dry) regions of the world the deserts are expanding. The dry seasons are lasting longer and in many areas the rains do not come when they should. The crops fail and people and animals die.

Greenhouse gases were in the atmosphere long before humans came along. One example is carbon dioxide, which is produced naturally by animals, plants and volcanoes. Indeed, without the natural greenhouse gases and greenhouse effect, the Earth's average surface temperature would be 33°C lower. Life as we know it could not exist. With the natural greenhouse effect, the Earth's average temperature had settled at around 15°C.

The problem today is that we are putting huge amounts of artificial greenhouse gases into the atmosphere. They will cause the world to overheat.

THE EARTH'S CHANGING TEMPERATURE

Since 1860, the Earth's average temperature has crept up by 0.5°C. Has the rise been the result of the extra greenhouse gases we have put into the atmosphere? It is difficult to be sure as there is a big natural variation in yearly temperatures. If we continue to produce as much of these gases as we do today, the average temperature could rise by about 1°C or more in just 30 years.

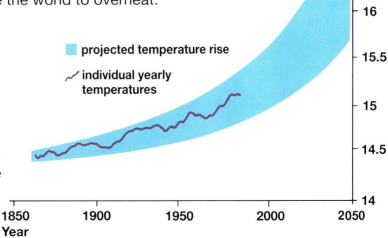

projected temperature rise

individual yearly temperatures

RATES OF WARMING

The Earth will warm up. A rise of 3°C by the year 2050 may not sound that much. The difference in average summer temperatures between London and Rome is 6°C. Between Boston and Washington in the USA, the difference is 4°C.

"THE BIG HEAT"

More than 200 of the world's climate scientists have been studying global warming. They concluded that if we keep making greenhouse gases at the rate we are today, the average temperatures will go up faster than at any time in 150,000 years.

CHANGES IN THE PAST

Let us look at how global average temperatures have altered during the past 15,000 years. These examples show just how important even a small change in global averages can be.

15,000-12,000 YEARS AGO
The world was in the grip of an Ice Age. The global average temperatures were up to 5°C lower than they are today. Huge ice sheets lay over much of Europe and North America. Mammoths and woolly rhinos were hunted by prehistoric people dressed in thick furs.

12,000-10,000 YEARS AGO
Average temperatures began to go up, as part of the natural climate cycle. The ice began to melt back towards the polar regions. Global temperatures were changing very fast, by about 1°C every 500 years.

10,000 YEARS AGO TO PRESENT
There has been very little change in global average temperatures. Sometimes the world was a bit warmer, and sometimes a bit cooler. It never differed by more than 1°C from today's global average of 15°C.

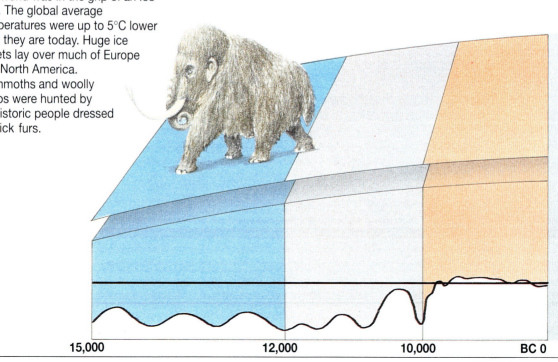

| 15,000 | 12,000 | 10,000 | BC 0 |

But remember that we are talking about global average temperatures. Compare 3°C in the next 50 to 100 years to the fastest natural change over the last 15,000 years: this happened at the end of the Ice Age, when the world warmed by about 1°C every 500 years. During this period, the cool-loving forests grew further north by a kilometre each year, to stay in a cool climate.

If the predictions for the next 50 years are correct, the rise in temperature will be at least 10 times faster than at the end of the Ice Age, and may be 100 times faster. Many biologists doubt that animals and plants will be able to adapt. Humans may cope for a time, but we depend on animals and plants in so many ways, from food and building materials to the oxygen we breathe.

MEDIEVAL WARM PERIOD
When the Vikings settled in Greenland (see page 11), in the late 10th century, the world temperature was slightly warmer than it is today, by around 0.5°C – yet Greenland was green and fertile.

THE "LITTLE ICE AGE"
In the 16th and 17th centuries, the world was slightly cooler, by about 0.5°C. London's River Thames, which never freezes over today, used to become frozen at that time. People held "frost fairs" and lit fires on the ice.

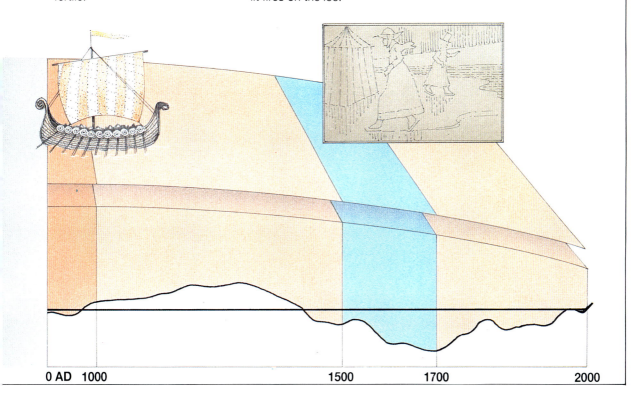

0 AD 1000   1500   1700   2000

RECIPE FOR DISASTER

As the greenhouse effect takes hold, planet Earth will undergo "global warming". This will have a great effect on the world. The seas and oceans, the polar ice caps, the weather, our cities and farmlands, and plants and animals everywhere will be affected.

Storms and droughts will increase. Warmer air will upset the global weather cycles and patterns. Hurricanes and cyclones will become more common and powerful, as has already happened in parts of the Caribbean and around India. Droughts will be more severe and widespread, leading to loss of crops and lives. The six warmest years this century have been in the 1980s. Who knows what the future holds?

HURRICANE ALERT

The numbers of strong hurricanes have increased in the past few years. This may be part of a natural cycle of weather patterns, but it may be the first signs of the greenhouse effect. Here, Hurricane Carol lashes the east coast of America causing a great deal of damage.

coastline
at present
sea level

flooded if sea
level rises by
4.6 metres

flooded if sea
level rises by
7.6 metres

Florida

Miami
beach

Gulf
of
Mexico

Keywest

RISING SEAS
The effect of a rise in sea level on the coastline of Florida.

ARE WE SURE?

Scientists cannot be sure what the greenhouse effect will bring because Nature is too complicated. On one hand, global warming could thaw the frozen Arctic tundra and release the methane gas trapped in the soil. Methane is one of the "greenhouse gases", so this could speed the greenhouse effect. On the other hand, global warming might lead to more clouds, which would shield the Earth and reflect more of the Sun's energy back into space. This would slow down the warming. These are just two examples of the many uncertainties.

COUNTDOWN

The results of the greenhouse effect may be here already.
- Hurricane Gilbert ripped through the West Indies in 1988.
- It was followed in 1989 by Hurricane Hugo, the strongest storm in the area for many years.
- In the 1980s, US farmers in the Midwest suffered two terrible droughts in a row.
- Unexpectedly high numbers of farmers in Italy and Spain have been made bankrupt because there is no water to irrigate their dry land.

The sea level will rise. Warmer air will make the water in the oceans expand. It will also melt the ice in glaciers and ice sheets, adding to the oceans' volume. Scientists predict that the sea levels will rise by 4 millimetres or more each year. This may not sound like much, but during the next century it will flood vast low-lying areas such as the coastal plains of Bangladesh, Egypt, Holland and eastern England, where millions of people live. Many of the world's capital cities are seaports, and they too will be affected.

Our food supply could be devastated. Rich farmland is often on low-lying coastal areas. As the seas flood the land, the salty water will seep into the soil and destroy its fertility. Droughts and storms will spoil the crops. If the sea rises by just 1 metre, one-sixth of today's farmland will disappear.

Plants and animals will be affected by the changing weather and extra warmth. Many will become extinct. Some will reproduce out of control and become pests as the temperature rises.

Much of this could be avoided, but only if we act at once to reduce the greenhouse effect, as explained on page 32. We have no choice.

THE GUILTY GASES

The artificial greenhouse gases, which are causing global warming, come from almost every kind of human activity. The gases are made by power stations and the energy industry, in factories and offices and homes, as we travel in cars, aircraft and trains, and during some types of farming.

It is clear that as we cut down on greenhouse gases, we will have to make changes to our lives and surroundings. These changes will affect almost everything we do.

It is also clear that the greenhouse gases are produced by many countries. So, the agreements about cutting down on their release will have to be truly international. This will involve enormous international co-operation (everyone working together), greater than the world has ever seen before.

WHICH GAS IS THE BIGGEST CULPRIT?

Which greenhouse gas is the most effective at trapping infrared heat, and so warming the atmosphere? This list shows the effectiveness of each one compared to carbon dioxide, the commonest "natural" greenhouse gas.

Carbon dioxide	1
Methane	20-60
Nitrous oxide	280
Ozone	2000
CFCs (see page 26)	10,000

WHO MAKES THE GASES?
Most greenhouse gases are produced by the wealthy industrial countries (see below). Yet the greenhouse effect will be worldwide.

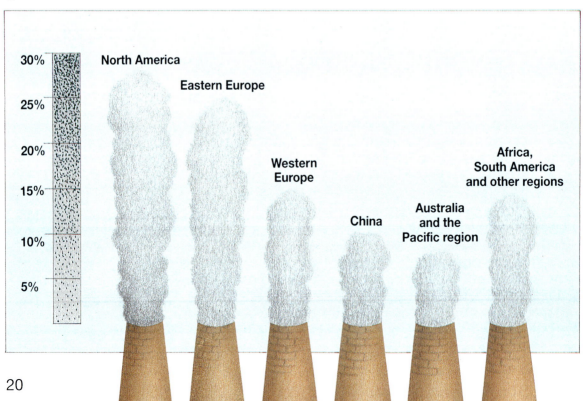

North America
Eastern Europe
Western Europe
China
Australia and the Pacific region
Africa, South America and other regions

30% 25% 20% 15% 10% 5%

CARBON DIOXIDE

- Concentration in atmosphere: 350 parts per million.
- Comes from: burning coal, petrol, gas and other fossil fuels; burning wood and forests; land erosion.
- Concentration in the year 2030 if we do not cut emissions: 460 parts per million.

METHANE

- Concentration in atmosphere: 1.7 parts per million.
- Comes from: fermentation in animal guts such as cattle (passed out as "wind"); fermentation in swamps, tundra and rice paddy-fields; rotting refuse; coal mines and gas leaks.
- Possible concentration in 2030: 2.7 parts per million.

NITROUS OXIDE

- Concentration in atmosphere: 0.3 parts per million.
- Comes from: fertilizer use; burning wood, forests, refuse and stubble.
- Possible concentration in the year 2030: 0.4 parts per million.

OZONE

- Concentration in atmosphere: 30–50 parts per billion.
- Comes from: chemical reactions in the air between gases such as carbon monoxide, nitrogen oxides and dust particles from car exhausts.
- Possible concentration in 2030: 150 parts per billion.

CFCs (chlorofluorocarbons)

- Concentration in atmosphere: 0.7 parts per billion.
- Come from: aerosols, fridge coolant fluids, air-conditioners, plastic foams and polystyrene cartons, chemical solvents.
- Possible concentration in 2030: 3 parts per billion.

ACID RAIN

Two main types of gas produce acid rain when they get into the atmosphere. These are sulphur dioxide and the nitrogen oxides, nitrogen dioxide and nitric oxide.

Most of these **acidifying** gases come from the burning of **fossil fuels** such as coal. Some go into the air as a result of natural processes in the sea, involving photosynthesis by microscopic plants called phytoplankton. The gases rise into the air and combine with water droplets in clouds to form acidic water. Sulphur dioxide makes sulphuric acid, while nitrogen oxides make nitric acid. In the clouds, other gases such as ammonia can speed the change from gas to acidic water.

When it rains, snows and hails, and when dew and frost form, the acids reach the ground. Here they damage the soil, the water in lakes and rivers, the wildlife, and even our buildings and machinery.

THE MAKING OF ACID RAIN

1. Power stations, factory chimneys, vehicle exhausts, heating boilers, house and cooking fires all produce acidic gases.
2. These gases rise into the air and dissolve in cloud water. Cloud water forms acidic rain droplets.
3. Acid rain is carried hundreds of kilometres by the wind.
4. Acid rain falls to the ground and soaks into the soil, damaging water, plants and animals.

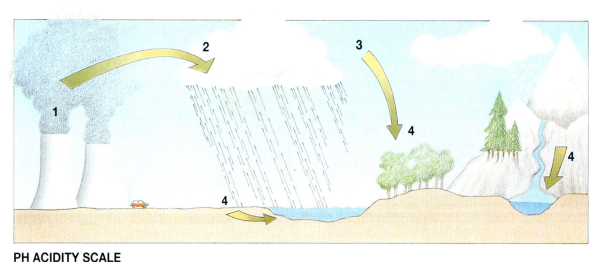

PH ACIDITY SCALE

London smog 1952   Acid rain   Pure rain

1	2	3	4	5	6	7	8	9	10	11	12	13	14

Acidic   Lemon juice   Neutral   Alkaline

DYING FISH

Acid rain washes tiny particles of the substance aluminium from the soil. The aluminium is swept into rivers and streams, where it interferes with the gills of fish, causing them to become clogged up and slimy. In Scandinavia, in the past 40 years, hundreds of lakes and rivers have lost all their fish – mostly trout and salmon. In 1900, 30,000 kilograms of salmon were caught in the seven largest rivers of southern Norway. Since 1970, no fish have been caught in these rivers.

DAMAGED BUILDINGS

Acid rain damages buildings and outdoor equipment such as playgrounds and farm machinery. In the USA, tens of billions of dollars are spent each year, mending buildings and repairing equipment affected by acid rain.

Many ancient monuments such as the Acropolis and the Mayan ruins in Mexico are being eaten away by acid rain. Famous statues and buildings, such as Gloucester Cathedral in England (above), show the erosion caused by acid rain and air pollution.

DYING TREES

Across Europe, and in many areas of North America, trees are being attacked by acid rain. Acidic water in the soil washes away the nutrients that the trees need to grow. It also causes their roots to take in aluminium, which is harmful. For example, in Holland, almost one-third of trees have lost many or most of their leaves. About two-thirds of British oak trees are seriously sick.

THE HUMAN TOLL

Breathing acidic air like this Mexico City "smog" can threaten health, especially for people who already have chest or lung illness. In the famous London "peasouper" smogs of the early 1950s, thousands of people died. The smogs were more acidic than lemon juice. This disaster resulted in the UK's Clean Air Act of 1956, which banned coal burning in the city, and improved London's air.

THE ACID WORLD

NORTH AMERICA

In the north-eastern USA, acidity is four times its level in 1900. This has happened at the same time as greater amounts of sulphur dioxide and nitrogen oxide gases were poured into the atmosphere. Canada has long complained to the USA that trees in Canadian forests are being harmed by acid rain from American industry.

TROPICS

Acid rain has even been found in the tropics, where there is very little industry. Here it comes largely from nitrogen oxides. These are released by wood burned in home and cooking fires, and by forests burned to make way for farmland and buildings.

The air of our atmosphere blows freely around the world. It does not stop at a country's borders, and it is not held back by the sea. So acidic gases and acidified water droplets in clouds are carried around the globe. Acid rain is becoming a worldwide problem.

Often, the countries that suffer are not the ones that make the acidic gases. They are "downwind" of the big acid-producers. One country's power stations, factories and car exhausts gradually ruin another's land, water and wildlife.

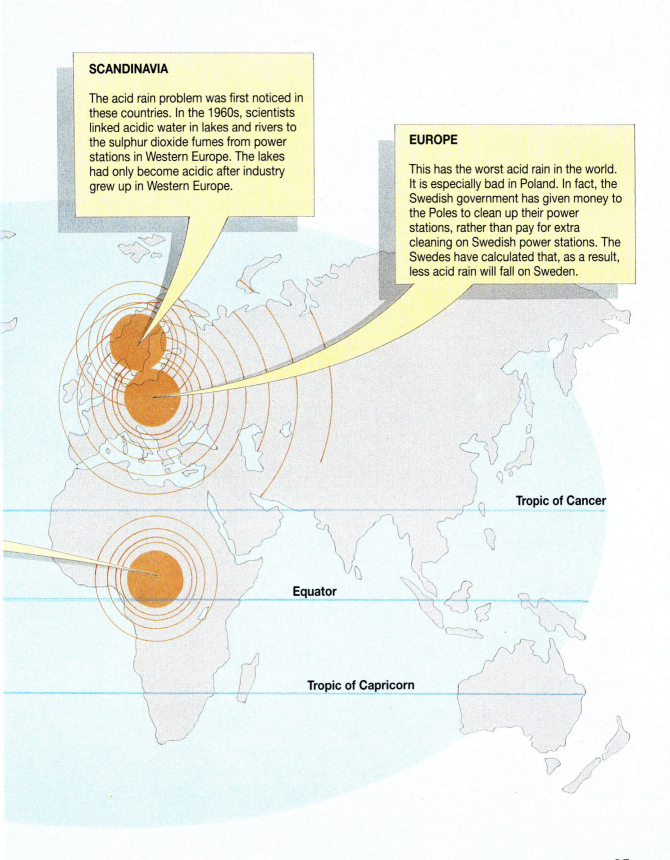

SCANDINAVIA

The acid rain problem was first noticed in these countries. In the 1960s, scientists linked acidic water in lakes and rivers to the sulphur dioxide fumes from power stations in Western Europe. The lakes had only become acidic after industry grew up in Western Europe.

EUROPE

This has the worst acid rain in the world. It is especially bad in Poland. In fact, the Swedish government has given money to the Poles to clean up their power stations, rather than pay for extra cleaning on Swedish power stations. The Swedes have calculated that, as a result, less acid rain will fall on Sweden.

Tropic of Cancer

Equator

Tropic of Capricorn

LOSS OF OZONE

In the 1930s, scientists invented chemicals called chlorofluorocarbons, or CFCs for short. For many years, these CFCs were thought to be wonderful substances. They did not react with other chemicals, and they had many uses in the cooling systems of refrigerators, aerosols, cleaning fluids, and as "blowing agents" for making foam-plastic boxes and packaging such as take-away food cartons. However, in a few years CFCs have changed from being useful industrial chemicals to becoming one of the main villains of the Air Scare.

The ozone layer, high in the atmosphere (see page 9), is vital to protect living things from the Sun's harmful ultraviolet rays. Yet there is not much ozone to do this. Although the layer stretches from about 20 to 50 kilometres above the Earth, the ozone is found only in tiny amounts, mixed up with other gases. If we could bring all that ozone down to the ground and spread it

HOW LONG WILL IT LAST?

CFCs can stay in the atmosphere for a hundred years. The CFCs that industry is putting into the atmosphere today, will still be destroying ozone in the year 2100. More and more CFCs are still going up into the atmosphere – the effects may last for centuries.

WHY ANTARCTICA?

There are clouds in the stratosphere over Antarctica. In these clouds are some of the coldest temperatures on Earth – as low as –80 °C. In the Antarctic winter, ice crystals form in the clouds. Chemical reactions on these ice crystals allow lots of chlorine to be released, ready to attack the ozone as soon as the first warmth of spring arrives.

WHERE IS NEXT?
We now know that CFCs are destroying ozone not only over Antarctica, but all around the Earth. Losses of almost one-tenth have been found at the same latitudes as Europe and North America. Scientists have also discovered big losses over the Arctic. An ozone hole, like the one over Antarctica, may develop there soon. The wildlife of both areas could be under threat. The effect on the polar bears of the Arctic (shown here) and the penguins of the Antarctic (see opposite on page 26) is not yet known.

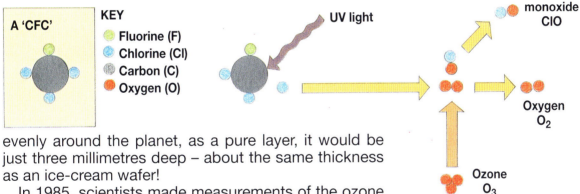

A 'CFC'

KEY
🟢 Fluorine (F)
🔵 Chlorine (Cl)
⚫ Carbon (C)
🔴 Oxygen (O)

UV light

Chlorine monoxide
ClO

Oxygen
O_2

Ozone
O_3

evenly around the planet, as a pure layer, it would be just three millimetres deep – about the same thickness as an ice-cream wafer!

In 1985, scientists made measurements of the ozone layer using high-altitude balloons and ground-based instruments. They found a "hole" in the ozone layer above Antarctica. We now know that, since about 1975, during each Antarctic spring (see caption opposite on page 26), almost half of the ozone has disappeared. It builds up again a few weeks later. This Antarctic ozone "hole" is the area of the USA, and as deep as Mount Everest is high.

What causes the loss of ozone? At first, scientists did not know. Then in 1987, a high-flying plane took samples of air in the stratosphere above Antarctica. The chemists analysed the air sample and soon they proved that CFCs were to blame.

HOW CFCs DESTROY OZONE
When CFC's are broken down by sunlight, they release chlorine. This is bad for ozone, a gas which is made of three oxygen atoms (O_3). Chlorine can steal one of these oxygen atoms, so turning ozone into normal oxygen (O_2). Worse, each chlorine atom can do this as many as 100,000 times.

EFFECTS OF OZONE LOSS

SEA LIFE

Life in the seas depends on tiny animals and plants that float in the surface waters – plankton (see below). Experiments have shown that plankton are badly affected by UV-B. Fish, which feed on plankton, will have less food. So will the people who rely on fish as their main source of protein.

The Sun's ultraviolet radiation has several forms. One, called UV-B, has very bad effects on living things. Normally, less than one-third of the UV-B reaching the Earth gets through to the surface. Now, with so much lost ozone, more UV-B is getting through.

UV-B causes sunburn and makes the skin wrinkled and "old". It also causes two types of skin cancer. One, malignant melanoma, can kill very quickly. The other, more common, type is called non-malignant, and the risk of death is lower. Skin cancers are most common in Australia, where light-skinned people live in a hot, sunny climate which is best suited for dark skin. (Black or dark skin has evolved to protect the body against the Sun's rays.) In the Australian state of Queensland, people develop malignant melanomas at ten times the rate they do in Britain. People who live all their lives in

PLANTS OF THE SEA

Many fish depend on plankton for their food. If the plankton die, so will the fish. The fishing catch will decline, affecting thousands of people.

Plankton numbers can be shown by satellite images (inset). Red shows that many are present, through yellow, green and blue to violet where there are few plankton.

DAMAGED CROPS
Tests have shown that plants are also affected by UV-B. What does this mean for our farmlands? Will they end up like these crops which have been exposed to drought?

WHAT THEY SAY

"Girls who wear bikinis or sunbathe nude in early adult life carry a risk of developing melanoma on the trunk 13 times greater than those who wear one-piece swimsuits. Adolescents with fair skin, fair hair and numerous freckles carry a risk 37 times greater than those with dark skin, dark hair and few freckles." British cancer expert, on the risks of skin cancers.

Queensland stand a 1-in-40 chance of developing melanoma, and a 1-in-150 chance of dying from it.

UV-B also causes cataracts, one of the main causes of blindness. Many thousands of people in undeveloped countries will become blind as a result of CFCs produced by developed countries. Some governments plan to produce even more CFCs. China wants its people to have a fridge in every home; and the fridges will almost certainly be cooled by chemicals containing CFCs rather than other coolants.

Perhaps the most worrying health effect is that UV-B may lower our resistance to disease. The rays interfere with the human body's immune system, which fights infection and protects us from illness. If the doctors' suspicions are proved, this will be a much more serious problem than skin cancers and cataracts.

WHAT WE MUST DO

In the future, the ozone loss means that more UV-B will be damaging life on Earth - at the same time as the planet is heating up as a result of the greenhouse effect. Remember that CFCs are also greenhouse gases (see page 21). Clearly, we have no choice but to stop the production of CFCs and other ozone-eating chemicals.

WHO CAN HELP?

People, governments and industries must work together if we are going to fix the atmosphere.

Many people, until now, did not understand just how bad things have become, but there are signs that opinions are changing. In many countries, surveys and opinion polls have shown that people are more and more worried about the environment, and especially about the state of the air we breathe. Ordinary people, if they act together, can use their votes to change government policies, and by only buying "safe" goods they can change industry's products.

Most governments, until now, have argued that it is a waste of time for one country to do anything on its own – what is known as **unilateral action**. This is because the threats are global. If one country cuts down on its greenhouse gases, acidifying gases and

PEOPLE POWER

Many people now feel very strongly about various environmental issues such as pollution and conservation (the protection of animals, plants and the environment). They often hold protest marches to try to persuade governments to change their policies.

ozone-eating gases, this will only have a small effect. However, environmental groups argue that such thinking is wrong. Each government must be brave and act by itself to cut down on harmful gases and so set an example to other governments.

Industries and the people who own them are obviously interested in making money. A company is unlikely to change its manufacturing methods and factory equipment in order to help the environment if this means it will lose money.

Governments are responsible for putting controls on the waste products that industries produce. These wastes include greenhouse gases, acidifying gases, and ozone-eating gases. Until now, government controls have not been strong enough. In the case of greenhouse gases, they are non-existent. This must change, and governments must tighten controls and prevent further damage to the atmosphere.

ECO-FRIENDLY INDUSTRY

Fortunately, some companies are becoming concerned about how they treat the environment. They are starting to sell "environment-friendly" products. This is because they believe that people are becoming very worried about the environment. They hope that customers will prefer to buy goods from companies whose methods are "kind" to the air, water and soil – even if the goods are slightly more expensive. This is why we see adverts for products like "ozone-friendly" aerosols, without CFCs.

CLEAN UP OUR AIR

The good news is this: we know exactly how to clean up and repair our atmosphere.

The bad news is this: doing it will involve major changes in the way we live. This is difficult, as many people still need to be persuaded of the need for change.

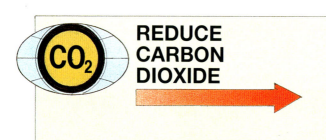

REDUCE CARBON DIOXIDE

We need targets for reducing carbon dioxide emissions (the amounts of carbon dioxide going into the air). The United States Environmental Protection Agency has shown that world emissions of carbon dioxide need to be cut by three-quarters to keep the carbon dioxide in the atmosphere stable (at the same level). But emissions go up year by year. In 1988, there were more than 20,000 million tonnes. Governments must set targets for reductions.

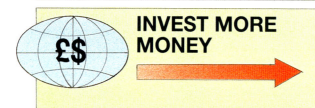

INVEST MORE MONEY

If the USA wanted to send a person to the moon today, like they did during the Apollo Project of the 1960s, it would cost over £150,000 million ($250 billion). We need to spend sums like this on vital action to survive the greenhouse effect and the heat trap.

USE DIFFERENT FORMS OF ENERGY

Rather than burning coal and other fossil fuels, which we cannot replace, we need to develop renewable forms of energy production. These include energy from the Sun (as solar power), wind and waves, which would produce little or no carbon dioxide (see page 36).

USE ENERGY MORE EFFICIENTLY

Our homes, schools, factories and offices all use up far more energy than they need. We must learn to use the most energy-efficient equipment, such as heaters, lights and machinery, which can use up to four-fifths less energy than the wasteful versions. We could also improve public transport so that people could travel easily without having to use cars all the time.

Governments will not take far-reaching and costly decisions, and so risk losing their elections, unless the people want change and vote for it.

To fix the greenhouse effect, we need to make the changes shown here. Acid rain and loss of ozone are dealt with on pages 30-31.

Will doing all this make our lives less comfortable? Many people believe not. There may be fewer luxury goods, less choice in the shops, fewer company cars, and so on. However, our quality of life will be much better. We will have cleaner air, better health, and hopefully more international cooperation and less war and conflict. In any event, if we want our children and grandchildren to have a better future, we have no choice.

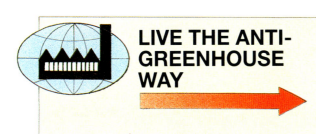

LIVE THE ANTI-GREENHOUSE WAY

We need encouragement and incentives for people and industry to use anti-greenhouse methods. We cannot trust the forces of business, commerce and the free market economy to repair the atmosphere. Governments will have to make laws that encourage people and industries to do the right things. For example, equipment that uses energy efficiently could have positive tax benefits or be sold for less than equipment that wastes energy.

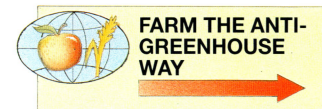

FARM THE ANTI-GREENHOUSE WAY

Organic farming – without artificial fertilizers – is the way of the future. It should enable us to cut down on the amounts of nitrous oxide that go into the atmosphere. We need to produce less methane, too. Less methane means far fewer cattle, sheep and goats.

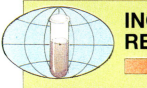

INCREASE RESEARCH

We should put more money into checking and research, so that we can understand better how nature works, and take the right actions in time to avoid an even worse tragedy.

STOP FOREST DESTRUCTION

Quick international action is vital to stop the cutting down of tropical forests. The former energy minister of Brazil calculated that it would cost over £1,600 million ($3,000 million) to save, and look after, two-thirds of the Amazon rainforests. This is the same amount that the USA will spend on just six of its B-2 "stealth" bombers.

CUT DOWN ON GASES

CUT DOWN ON ACIDIC GASES

Governments should agree to cut emissions of sulphur dioxide by nine-tenths, and of nitrogen oxides by three-quarters. Scientists have shown that only such drastic cuts will help to restore the atmosphere and reduce the risks to plants, trees and animals.

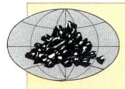

REDUCE COAL-FIRED POWER PLANTS

Power stations that burn coal in order to generate electricity are the main problem. They produce most of the sulphur dioxide and nitrogen oxides which make acid rain. We already know that we need far fewer coal-fired power stations if we are to fight global warming. So we can improve the atmosphere in two ways.

FILTER POWER-PLANT FUMES

Filters are needed for the coal-fired power stations that remain. These filters can remove more than nine-tenths of the sulphur emissions from the smoke coming out of the chimney stacks. They would cut down acid rain dramatically. However, governments have been slow, even on agreeing to fit these filters. For example, Britain has over 40 coal and other fossil-fuel power stations, but it has only agreed to fit filters to three, by the year 2003. Other governments are more strict. In 1983, West Germany decided to cut its acidic power-station fumes by four-fifths in six years after finding that its forests were badly affected by acid rain. The cost will be nearly £10,000 million.

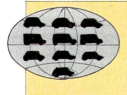

HAVE FEWER CARS AND TRUCKS

Fumes from vehicle exhausts are a major source of the nitrogen oxides that lead to acid rain. In 1950, there were 50 million cars in the world. Now there are nearly 400 million. By the end of the century, if we do not cut back, there will be around 500 million. Environmental groups point out that this is a form of suicide. We already know that we need fewer cars in order to cut down fuel-burning and so tackle the greenhouse effect. Again, we can tackle two Air Scare problems if we use fewer cars and trucks.

CAN WE MAKE THE WORLD FAIRER?

At present, developed countries make money out of less-developed countries. This is because these countries pay back millions of pounds on loans made to them by rich countries. In the future, the richer countries will have to help the developing countries to feed themselves, beginning by giving them equipment for the efficient use of energy. They can also "write off" or "forget" the millions of pounds which the less developed countries owe to banks in industrialized countries. At present, much of the money raised by cutting down tropical forests is used to pay back these debts.

BAN OZONE-DAMAGING CHEMICALS

We should be aiming for a worldwide ban on the production of all ozone-damaging substances. These include chemicals like methyl chloroform and carbon tetrachloride, and not just the CFCs and others listed in the Montreal Protocol (see page 12).

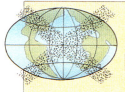

BAN EXPORT OF CFCs

There is no point in stopping the use of CFCs in your own country, if you still export them to other countries. Britain has agreed to the terms of the Montreal Protocol on this subject. British companies still make CFCs and export them to countries which have not signed the Protocol. A ban on the sale of CFCs from one country to another would stop this.

FIT "CATALYTIC CONVERTERS"

"Three-way catalytic converters" are special boxes which fit into the exhaust pipes of cars and trucks. They reduce nitrogen oxide emissions by up to nine-tenths. In the USA, these have been fitted to all new cars since 1981. In Europe, they are required by law in several countries. Britain has agreed to fit them to all new cars after 1992. People who really need a car can drive a car with a "three-way cat". The use of lead-free fuel should also be encouraged by making it cheaper than other petrol by lower taxes. Finally, in future, cars should be made to run on batteries, solar panels or other methods that do not use petrol.

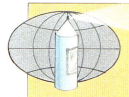

END CFC PRODUCTION

We should end CFC production immediately in all products not just aerosols. We must not take as much notice of "the needs of industry" as we have done in the past. Industry can, and must, use alternatives to CFCs. The alternatives may cost more, and they may be less convenient, but we must make industry use them by public pressure.

ENERGY FROM CARBON

We all use energy every day. Driving a car, switching on a light, turning on the water heater, cooking a meal, and lighting the fire all use energy. Industries use vast amounts of energy, especially as electricity.

The rich industrialized countries make about nine-tenths of their energy by burning coal, oil, natural gas – so-called fossil fuels. This releases enormous amounts of carbon dioxide into the atmosphere. For example, every tonne of coal burned – in a power station or in an ordinary house – produces about two-and-a-half tonnes of carbon dioxide. The average car burns so much petrol in one year that it puts four times its own weight of carbon dioxide into the atmosphere.

A quick look at the sums shows that this cannot continue. Coal, oil and gas, and the carbon dioxide they produce when burned, all contain the chemical

ENERGY FROM COAL
Coal-fired power stations are used to generate most of the electricity used in the UK.

WORLD USE OF FOSSIL FUELS

We use far more coal, oil and gas today than we did in the 1930s. The graph shows how many billions of tonnes of carbon there are in the carbon dioxide released.

ENERGY SOURCES

Energy can come from coal, oil, wind, waves and tides, hydro-energy (from moving water) and gases from rotting plants and animals. Energy sources and use for a typical industrialized country and a less developed one are shown below.

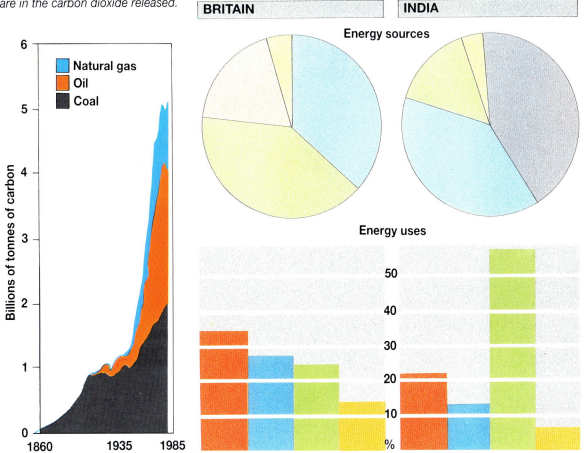

element carbon (C). Now, consider the atmosphere in terms of the amount of carbon it contains. Before industry, when the world's atmosphere was safe and stable, it contained about 570,000 million tonnes of carbon. Now it contains 740,000 million tonnes. This is because we have added extra carbon each year, from coal-burning power stations, petrol-burning cars and diesel-burning trucks.

We know roughly how much fossil fuel is left in the ground. It amounts to some 10 million million tonnes. If we do not stop burning it, global warming will speed up even more, and bring us nearer to a worldwide catastrophe. We need to encourage forms of renewable energy, as explained on the next two pages.

KEY

Energy source
- Coal
- Oil
- Natural gas
- Nuclear and hydroelectric
- Wood and wastes

Energy use
- Industry
- Transport
- Household
- Others

RENEWABLE ENERGY

Renewable forms of energy are those that will not run out – at least, not while the Sun shines. The Sun provides us with useable energy, both directly (as sunshine), and as the driving force behind our weather (see page 10). The main forms of renewable energy are solar power, wave and tide power, wind power and hydroelectric power from running water. These are good for the atmosphere because they produce no carbon dioxide. **Geothermal energy** from the Earth's core can also be used. The energy produced by burning **biomass**, for example wood, plant matter and animal dung, is also important, especially in undeveloped countries.

Renewable energy has some way to go before it can provide us with the same quantities of energy that the fossil fuels give us today. Can it be done? Some scientists, but by no means all, think it can. To be successful, we must keep the world's energy needs at today's levels, and not allow them to increase. With a growing world population, and undeveloped countries just beginning to develop industries, this will mean hard work, and plenty of money to spend on energy efficiency.

US ENERGY CONSUMPTION

Like all industrialized societies, the United States uses a great deal of energy. As shown below, most of this energy is obtained from coal, oil and gas.

Total world energy production from various sources in 1988 was: oil, 33%; coal, 27%; natural gas, 18%; renewables, 17%; nuclear, 5%.

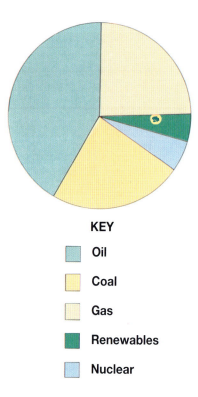

KEY

- Oil
- Coal
- Gas
- Renewables
- Nuclear

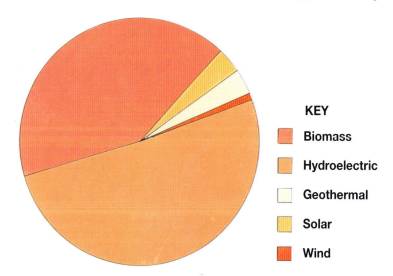

KEY

- Biomass
- Hydroelectric
- Geothermal
- Solar
- Wind

US SOURCES OF RENEWABLE ENERGY

As can be seen from the chart above, most of the energy in the US comes from oil and coal. Less than 8% of its energy comes from renewables. Most renewable energy comes from hydroelectric power and burning biomass. Despite the widespread use of solar heating, it provides only about 1% of the total renewable energy used. There is obviously room for improvement.

SUNLIGHT

Solar panels contain chemicals and electronic circuits that trap heat and turn it into electricity. Present-day panels are useful only in very sunny places, such as parts of Australia, the United States and the Middle East. Further research is needed to make them more efficient.

TIDES

Tidal energy comes originally from the gravitational pull of the Sun and Moon. It is an endless source of energy, but the barrages or dams needed to capture it would spoil the natural scenery. They would also alter the pattern of water flow and disturb seabirds, fish and other shore life.

The movement of the waves compresses, or squashes up, the air. The pressure produced turns the turbine engine

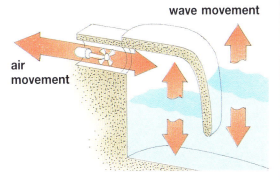

wave movement

air movement

WIND

The energy in moving air came originally from the Sun (see page 14). "Wind parks" or "farms" of huge windmills have been built in a few places. They can generate enough electricity to run a small town. However, they only work in windy areas, and they are unsightly and can ruin the natural landscape.

WAVES

Wind whips up waves on the oceans. The energy of the moving water could be turned into electricity using special floating rafts or barrages. However, the equipment would have to be extremely strong to withstand constant battering by the waves and corrosion by salt water. Also, the generating station would be a blot on the coastline.

NUCLEAR ENERGY

TROJAN POWER
The Trojan nuclear power plant in Oregon in the United States has a power output of 1 million kilowatts – twice the hydroelectric power made by the Bonneville Dam.

WHERE TO PUT THE WASTES?

Nuclear power stations produce a lot of radioactive wastes, from the highly dangerous fuel rods to the slightly contaminated protective clothes of the workers. We have failed so far to find a truly safe place to store the high level waste. The radioactivity will last for thousands of years. If it gets into the environment, it could have horrifying effects.

Nuclear power produces little carbon dioxide but it also has many drawbacks. Can it become a major source of energy in the future? There are many heated arguments about this subject.

Some people say that, because of the numerous safety problems, nuclear power can have little or no role in the future. There are about 400 nuclear power stations in the world today. If all the electricity now generated by burning coal was generated instead by nuclear power, we would need more than 4000 nuclear power stations! Even if this happened, as coal-fired power stations only produce about one-tenth of all greenhouse gases (see page 20), nine-tenths of the greenhouse gases would remain.

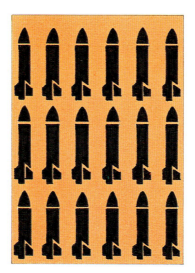

AT THE END OF ITS LIFE ...?

When a nuclear power station comes to the end of its working life, what should be done with it? Dismantling a station is a long, tricky and dangerous procedure. We have yet to see the first nuclear power station successfully decommissioned or dismantled. How can all the leftover parts be made safe? There are no answers at present.

MORE NUCLEAR WEAPONS?

A few of the existing reactors have provided enough nuclear material to build many nuclear bombs, missiles and other weapons. This could allow countries which do not have nuclear bombs at present to build their own weapons. Does the world really need more nuclear arms?

SAFETY

There have been three major accidents at nuclear power stations already – including the terrifying Chernobyl disaster. Doctors say that many thousands of people will die from cancer as a result of the accident at Chernobyl. A world with 4000 nuclear reactors would be an even less safe place.

In any case, the extra 3600 nuclear power stations could not be built fast enough to deal with the greenhouse effect. It takes at least six years to build one, and many countries could not afford the money or materials. There are also many worries about the safety of nuclear power (see above). Finally, these stations would cost thousands of billions of pounds to build. The money would give much better value if it were invested in renewable energy and using energy more efficiently.

Other people argue that nuclear power is the way forward. They say that the safety and waste problems can be solved. They also say that there will be grave risks of power cuts and lack of electricity supplies if we rely on renewable energy (see page 38).

THE TOP THREE

- USA – 99 reactors; 21 being built; 17% of national electricity output.
- USSR – 50 reactors; 32 being built; 10% of national electricity output.
- France – 49 reactors; 14 being built; 70% of national electricity output.

HOW WE CAN ALL HELP

It is up to us all to help take care of our environment. There are many ways in which individuals can take positive steps to cut down on the chemical pollutants that are destroying our atmosphere. Governments and businesses can also make a large impact – it is just a matter of "thinking green".

One of the most important steps to take is to cut down on the total amount of energy used in the world. Look at the checklist below and see how you, your family and friends can help by conserving energy both at home and at work and by buying "environmentally friendly" goods. Even the smallest action by an individual can help to solve the problem and clean up our atmosphere.

LOCAL GOVERNMENT

● Assess potential impact of policies and actions on the local area, eg coastal protection and natural ecosystems

● Ban the use of CFCs in all packaging, insulation and aerosols

● Organize and finance planting of trees, especially deciduous woodland trees

● Encourage and develop plans to use renewable energy

● Use savings from energy conservation to set up a special "Greenhouse" fund to protect the environment

● Provide recycling centres for CFCs. Make sure that CFCs from old refrigerators and freezers are salvaged and recycled

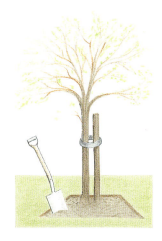

ENERGY

● Insulate the loft, cavity walls and water tank in your home

● Fit draught-stripping to doors and windows

● Use energy efficient light bulbs and electrical appliances

● Fit thermostats to radiators

TRANSPORT

● Use public transport whenever possible

● Share your car on trips to work and school

● Choose a fuel-efficient, low-polluting car

● Walk or use a bicycle for short trips

PAPER/TREES

- Buy goods made of recycled paper

- Avoid disposable products and refuse excess packaging like plastic and paper bags

- Plant trees

- Avoid goods made from rare tropical hardwoods which do not have a "Good Wood" seal of approval and are made from specially grown trees

CONSUMER POWER

- Buy goods locally

- Buy only CFC-free aerosols and polystyrene

- Boycott companies involved in the destruction of tropical rainforests – do not buy their goods

- Write to chemical companies still producing ozone-damaging and greenhouse chemicals and ask them to stop

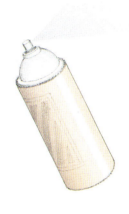

CAMPAIGNING

- Join an environmental group

- Write letters to your MP and local newspaper

- Get your local council to plant more trees and save energy

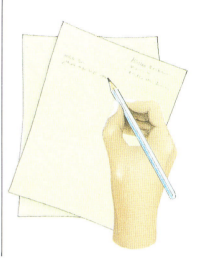

FOOD

- Eat less meat

- Buy organic food which has not been treated with pesticides or inorganic fertilizers

BUSINESS

- Assess use of CFCs and production of other "greenhouse gases" in your industry and set targets to reduce output

- Develop a company policy on environmental issues such as the production of "greenhouse gases"

- Change vehicle fleet to high-efficiency vehicles which use lead-free petrol and/or catalytic converters (cats)

- Help developing countries to establish the use of modern technology which does not involve production of atmospheric pollutants

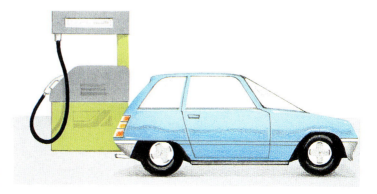

GLOSSARY

Acid rain   Rain, dew, or snow which is more acidic than is usual. Acid rain is produced by the sulphur dioxide and nitrogen oxides that are given off when fossil fuels are burned.

Acidifying   A chemical that can turn water into an acid.

Atmosphere   The envelope of air (a mixture of gases) that blankets planet Earth.

Biomass   The mass of organic material produced as a result of life. We can use this word, for example, for all wood produced by trees, or all the wastes produced by animals, and even for the organic matter in the animals themselves.

Climate   The weather conditions typically experienced in an area over periods of years.

Corrosive   A substance, like an acid, that can wear away an object as a result of a chemical reaction.

Fossil fuels   Coal, oil and gas are all fossil fuels. They are all made of carbon, and if you burn them you get carbon dioxide (a greenhouse gas) and the gases that produce acid rain.

Geothermal energy   Heat that is tapped from deep in the Earth.

Global warming   The heating up of the Earth's atmosphere as a result of the greenhouse effect.

Greenhouse effect   The trapping in the atmosphere of infrared radiation from the Earth's surface. Greenhouse gases do this.

Infrared radiation   A type of radiation that cannot be seen, and that transmits heat. The Earth's surface is heated by solar radiation, for example, and gives off infrared radiation. When you eat food, your bodies produce energy, so giving off infrared radiation.

Mesosphere   The region of the atmosphere between 50 and 80 kilometres up, which separates the stratosphere from the thermosphere.

Ozone   A gas similar to oxygen, which is most common in the ozone layer. The ozone layer is in the stratosphere, and protects living things from ultraviolet radiation from the Sun.

Photosynthesis   A process used by plants to make food. They add carbon dioxide to water using the energy of sunlight.

Radiation   A general word for rays, waves, or particles from a source. Solar radiation, for example, is the release of various types of radiation (all travelling at the speed of light) from the Sun.

Reflect   When rays of light hit an object they bounce back off. This is called reflection.

Respiration   The way in which living things obtain energy from food. During this process oxygen is used up, and carbon dioxide is released.

Stratosphere   The region of the atmosphere between about 10 to 15 and 50 kilometres up, which separates the troposphere from the mesosphere. It contains the ozone layer.

Trace gases   Gases that make up only a tiny proportion of all the gas in the atmosphere. Greenhouse gases are trace gases.

Thermosphere   The region of the atmosphere, from about 80 to 400 kilometres up, where temperatures increase with height.

Troposphere   The lowest layer of the atmosphere, ending about 10 to 15 kilometres up. It is the "weather zone", where the air is densest, where almost all clouds form, and where temperature decreases with height.

Ultraviolet radiation   A type of solar radiation which cannot be seen but which can hurt living things if they are exposed to too much of it. It causes sunburn, for example.

Unilateral action   An action taken by a country (usually we use this word for a good action) without waiting to see if other countries will do the same. Some countries are considering unilaterally cutting the amounts of greenhouse gases they put into the atmosphere, in order to slow global warming.

Visible radiation   A type of solar radiation that we can see.

Weather   The conditions of temperature, rainfall and wind experienced by an area on a day-to-day basis.

FURTHER READING

For Children
Pollution and the Environment by M. Lean;
MacDonald Children's Books, 1985.
Air Ecology by J. Cochrane; Project Ecology;
Wayland, 1987.
Acid Rain by J. Baines; Conserving Our World;
Wayland, 1989.
The Young Green Consumer Guide by J. Elkington
and J. Hailes; Victor Gollancz Ltd, 1990.

For Adults
The Gaia Atlas of Planet Management by N. Myers
(editor); Pan Books, 1985.
The Greenhouse Effect by S. Boyle and J. Ardill;
New English Library, 1989.
The Greenpeace Story by Michael Brown and John
May; Dorling Kindersley, 1989.

USEFUL ADDRESSES

Department of the Environment (DoE)
2, Marsham Street, London SW1
The DoE has many leaflets and guidelines on
environmental issues.

Council for Environmental Education
School of Education, University of Reading,
London Road, Reading, Berks RG1 5AQ
Helps youth organizations to learn more about the
environment.

Friends of the Earth (FoE)
26–28 Underwood Street, London N1
FoE is an action group that organizes campaigns on
environmental issues. They have a youth section,
Earth Action, for people aged 14 to 23.

Greenpeace UK
30–31 Islington Green, London N1 8XE
Greenpeace organizes protests and campaigns
against the destruction of the environment. They also
present scientific information on various
environmental projects to many governments. They
will answer questions and give advice to
organizations and schoolchildren who write to them.

Waste Watch
National Council for Voluntary Organizations,
26 Bedford Square, London WC1B 3HU
Details of environmental groups and voluntary
organizations in the UK are available from Waste
Watch.

WATCH Trust for Environmental Education Ltd
22 The Green, Nettleham, Lincoln LN2 2NR
WATCH works with schools and helps to organize
conservation projects. It aims to increase knowledge
of the natural world and encourage conservation.

World Wide Fund for Nature (WWF)
Panda House, Weyside Park, Godalming,
Surrey GU7 1XR
WWF encourages the conservation of plants and
animals throughout the world.

INDEX